Chicken

by
Mike Batistick

Playdead Press

Published by Playdead Press 2012

© Mike Batistick 2012

Mike Batistick has asserted his rights under the Copyright, Design and Patents Act, 1988, to be identified as the author of this work.

A CIP catalogue record for this book is available from the British Library.

ISBN 978-0-9572859-2-7

Caution
All rights whatsoever in this play are strictly reserved and application for performance should be sought through the author before rehearsals begin. No performance may be given unless a license has been obtained.

This book is sold subject to the condition that it shall not by way of trade or otherwise, be lent, resold, hired out, or otherwise circulated without the publisher's prior consent in any form of binding or cover other than that in which it is published and without a similar condition including this condition being imposed on the subsequent purchaser.

Playdead Press
www.playdeadpress.com

Michael Batistick is the author of three critically acclaimed Off-Broadway plays, including CHICKEN. His film PONIES will make its theatrical premiere in New York in July. His television pilot WE COUNTED YOUR KNIVES is currently in development at NBC Universal/USA Networks.

Inner City Productions was founded in 2008. Born from a director and actor collaboration, the realization soon became apparent that the need to reflect creative outsiders from ALL walks of life, not just those in vogue, was a loud and urgent calling. From story tellers to writers, from directors to camera operators, from thespians to movie stars. Each person brings with them their own creative path, filled with a rich tapestry of traditions and culture that, if given the support and opportunity, can offer a unique and fresh approach to new and challenging work. Inner City also see the need to look back in order to inspire the leaps forward so believes bringing classics to the stage, again from those outsiders that have not been showcased enough in London, is the key to changing the system of stereotyping cultures to their skin tone, accent and sexuality. Breaking the cultural moulds that have set is our goal and we aim to reflect this in all aspects of our work.

The author would like to wish special thanks to Sam Neophytou, George Georgiou, and the crew at Inner City Productions for their continued belief in this play and my work. Also, a hearty shout out to Michael Imperioli, Nick Sandow, and the gone-but-not-forgotten Studio Dante in New York City.

Chicken was first performed in the UK by Innercity Productions in Spring 2000 at Theatro Technis, London. The cast was as follows:

Floyd	George Georgiou
Wendall	Jimmy Roussounis
Lina	Mitzi Jones
Geronimo	David Lee Jones
Felix	Morgan Deare
Rosalind	Sinead Beary
Director	Sam Neophytou

Chicken received its West End Premiere performed by Innercity productions at The Trafalgar Studio 2, London on 25th June 2012. The cast was as follows:

Floyd	George Georgiou
Wendall	Craig Kelly
Lina	Lisa Maxwell
Geronimo	Daniel Yabut
Felix	Andy Lucas
Rosalind	Amy Tez
Director	Sam Neophytou

Chicken

by
Mike Batistick

CAST OF CHARACTERS

WENDELL: An unhealthy man

FLOYD: His longtime friend, wiry

LINA: Wendell's wife, six and half months pregnant

GERONIMO: A Filipino neighbor

FELIX: Floyd's dad

ROSALIND: Floyd's estranged wife

SETTING
The Bronx, not far from Fordham Road and Webster Avenue

TIME
Present Day

SCENE 1

Setting: A cramped apartment in the Bronx. Early afternoon. Across much of the down and mid-stage—stacked both ankle and knee-high—are piles of envelopes, piles of papers, and several piles of junk.

*At rise, **WENDELL**, an unhealthy looking man, stares at a rooster, which sits in a container below him. **FLOYD**, his friend, stands nearby.*

WENDELL	*(To **FLOYD**)* He's a little sick. So he has to stay downstairs for a little while.
FLOYD	Ok.
WENDELL	Yeah. Once he's better, he'll go on the roof. With the other ones. Upstairs.
FLOYD	Other ones?
WENDELL	There are four more of them. On the roof.
FLOYD	Lina is gonna kill you.
WENDELL	The healthy ones are in the homing pigeon cages right now. But he's 'spose to be the best one, why isn't he healthy Floyd?
FLOYD	You need to get this bird out of the apartment.
WENDELL	He might die if he goes outside right now.
FLOYD	He's sitting here being sick in your living room.
WENDELL	So?

FLOYD What if he gives us what he's got? What if he dies in here?

WENDELL Why are you saying that?

FLOYD Look at him. You can't just bring these things into your home. He's so sick, they've got stuff on them.

WENDELL You don't know that.

FLOYD Didn't you at least ask why he looks so bad?

WENDELL I think it happens sometimes.

FLOYD Yeah. It just happens sometimes when you die. Why didn't you ask me about it before you bought it?

WENDELL I didn't buy it.

FLOYD Then where'd you get this thing?

WENDELL Geronimo.

FLOYD *(Beat)* What?

WENDELL Geronimo.

FLOYD You're kiddin', right?

WENDELL Look, I know you're still pissed at him.

FLOYD Pissed at him?

WENDELL You gotta get over this Floyd.

FLOYD Pissed at him? He's the reason I'm in this situation in the first place.

WENDELL All you had to do was patch up old tires and help him raise the chickens in the back and he still let you go.

FLOYD He should be deported.

WENDELL Look, I'm sorry he fired you, but welcome to one of his birds. *(Beat)* Floyd. You

	know you can stay here as long as you want, but like… you can't, either.
FLOYD	My dad would think you're insane bringin' a bird in the house.
WENDELL	Speakin' of your dad—
FLOYD	I was not speakin' of my dad—
WENDELL	I called him up. He gave me a recipe to condition this thing. Like a diet plan. He said you'd know how to put it together right.
FLOYD	You called him up?
WENDELL	Yeah. He sorta ran out of juice towards the end, I didn't get the whole thing, and he's really hard to understand now, but he said you'd know how to administer it. Maybe you can call him up and get the rest of it. It's a morning-of thing, to get the birds excited before the fight.
FLOYD	Wendell?
WENDELL	What?
FLOYD	What are you doing?
WENDELL	*(Hard for HIM)* Lina's about to pop with the baby, Floyd. You been loafin' on my couch for like three months. I got no fucking money left, her belly is getting bigger and bigger. You're gonna train this bird and then you're movin' out with the money.
FLOYD	*(Beat)* Wendell. I got nowhere to go.
WENDELL	I'll help you find somewhere.

4

FLOYD   Wendell—

WENDELL   Thirty five thousand if we win. You're the half Cuban, your people's DNA is built for this shit, you're the only person I know who even knows how to look at a fighting rooster.

FLOYD   Wendell—

WENDELL   Its in Washington Heights, Geronimo sucks at winning these things, he hasn't won since you left, you gotta do this Floyd. *(Beat)* Then you gotta move out.

FLOYD   When you're baby girl comes you're gonna ask yourself again and again why you didn't reach for that rubber two trimesters ago. A cockfight's not gonna help things.

WENDELL   Yeah it will.

FLOYD   This shit's illegal.

WENDELL   Illegal?

FLOYD   Don't you work for, like, the city?

WENDELL   So?

FLOYD   You should have ethics.

WENDELL   I collect tolls all day on the Whitestone Bridge. Ethics?

FLOYD   I got a strong feeling you're only shooting girl bullets.

WENDELL   Excuse me?

FLOYD   There is no doubt that your child is a girl. Look at the way you're behavin'. Take this piece-of-poultry-shit back to

	Geronimo and his smelly tire pile of a tire shop and just let it go.
WENDELL	Floyd—
FLOYD	Filipino gypsy. He's gettin' in your head.
WENDELL	How?
FLOYD	Like he did. When we were kids.
WENDELL	He just wants you to show up to work on time.
FLOYD	Back of his tire shop hatchin' roosters so he can fight in Washington Heights? Filipinos: they do curses on you. He did his flip gypsy curse all over you and this bird. Putting his sad, third world face on, jealous we speak English better, I'm glad I quit his shop—
WENDELL	You got fired—
FLOYD	This bird's a mutt, look at it. It's sick. Any bird that's ever come outta the back a that shop that ever worked I built. I did not have a hand in this thing, I do not make sick birds.
WENDELL	Floyd.
FLOYD	What?
WENDELL	Apparently this thing is modified.
FLOYD	*(Beat)* What?
WENDELL	He's enhanced. He's special.
FLOYD	What are you talkin' about?
WENDELL	Geronimo has added specifications. To his genes.
FLOYD	What? How?

WENDELL	He got a hold of some hormone. He put it in both bird's parents. His four brothers are just like him. Go look on the roof. They're huge. Plus you gotta see his moms.
FLOYD	(*Interested, but trying to hide it*) She big?
WENDELL	His moms looks like Nell Carter.
FLOYD	What?
WENDELL	Yeah. Like Gimme A Break.
FLOYD	Wendell. Having a mom like Nell Carter, Wendell, I don' know if that's . . .
WENDELL	What?
FLOYD	Positive.
WENDELL	Sure it is.
FLOYD	Nell Carter's heart stopped at like forty.
WENDELL	(*Beat*) Floyd. This thing's a Calagay.
FLOYD	A what?
WENDELL	A Calagay fighting rooster from Calagay, France.
FLOYD	France.
WENDELL	Yeah.
FLOYD	Like, Europe?
WENDELL	Yeah, like France. Calagay, France.

(*FLOYD examines the rooster more closely, perhaps approaching the cage*)

FLOYD	France, huh?
WENDELL	Yeah. France.

FLOYD How'd Nimo get him over here if he's from France?
WENDELL Things from France are sophisticated.
FLOYD Listen to you, you already sound like him.
WENDELL Well it's true. France is classy.
FLOYD You're a native born American and you just sounded like the City of Manilla. "France is sophisticated," I can hear him sayin' it.
WENDELL You walk outside today Floyd? Half of Haiti lives out there now there's so much French.
FLOYD So?
WENDELL You want to let these people beat you? This is your country.
FLOYD This country put me in an orphanage.
WENDELL Poor fucking baby. Me too.
FLOYD Don't we have enough roosters over here that we don't have to import them from France?
WENDELL A chicken is a chicken.
FLOYD No. A chicken is a girl chicken. A rooster is a boy chicken. All of them are birds. A chicken is not just a chicken, no wonder Geronimo conned you.
WENDELL Cut his feathers, Floyd. We're gonna at least make him look good if he's gonna get his ass kicked.
FLOYD That's the entirely wrong attitude to have, you thinking he's gonna get his ass kicked.

WENDELL	Cut his feathers like a fighting bird then I'll think whatever you want. I'll get you vitamins and supplements, you're gonna cut his feathers, you're gonna train this bird, then you're moving out.
FLOYD	No I'm not.
WENDELL	Yes you are.
FLOYD	I'm staying right here.
WENDELL	Stop pretending like you live here.
FLOYD	I do live here.
WENDELL	No. You. Don't.

(Pause)

FLOYD	*(A bit scared)* You're serious.
WENDELL	Like a big piece of cancer.

*(Another pause. **FLOYD** examines the bird some more)*

FLOYD	I gotta say.
WENDELL	What?
FLOYD	It's a very handsome rooster.
WENDELL	*(Beat)* It is, isn't it?
FLOYD	Yeah. So he's modified.
WENDELL	Yeah. He's modified. From another continent. *(Beat)* Floyd, I am so not fucking around with this. *(Beat)* I'm going to get something to eat. I'm starving.
FLOYD	We just ate.
WENDELL	I'm hungry.

FLOYD	How?
WENDELL	I appreciate it, you cutting his feathers.
FLOYD	No problem.
WENDELL	These things are so depressing until somebody cuts their feathers.
FLOYD	Probably gonna be depressing afterwards too.
WENDELL	No. From here on out we talk positive. I'm goin' to get food. That's positive. Five French birds. That's positive. This chicken—
FLOYD	Rooster—
WENDELL	The rooster. Is positive. The entire planet is going to be a radioactive glow of positivity from here on out, okay?
FLOYD	*(Beat)* Okay.
WENDELL	Thank you for agreeing to cut his feathers.
FLOYD	No problem.
WENDELL	Just make sure you do it on the roof.

SCENE 2

Setting: The same day. Late afternoon. The apartment.

At rise, the ROOSTER looks different now, its feathers have been impressively cut. A bag of McDonald's sits on the kitchen table. LINA, Wendell's pregnant wife, keeps a safe distance from the rooster. SHE cannot believe what she is seeing. WENDELL tries to explain.

LINA　　　　　Are you kidding me?

WENDELL　　I was gonna move it. Why are you home so early?

LINA　　　　　'Cause I'm pregnant. 'Cause my ankles hurt. 'Cause I threatened to sue Macy's if they didn't let me take a car service home for a minute—why is there a rooster in my living room?

WENDELL　　You gotta go back again tonight?

LINA　　　　　How many times I gotta tell you: perfume is eternal. *(Back to the ROOSTER)* What the fuck is this?

WENDELL　　I can explain.

LINA　　　　　You better.

WENDELL　　I brought it home for Floyd, so he'd train it and move out with the money.

LINA　　　　　They completely carry bacteria.

WENDELL　　Who?

LINA　　　　　Birds.

WENDELL　　No they don't. Where'd you hear that?

LINA　　　　　Move him outta the way. I gotta get to the kitchen.

WENDELL　　You can get around it, just walk around him.

LINA　　　　　Him?

WENDELL　　It's a boy.

LINA　　　　　There's shit everywhere, I got enough shit cluttering up my life, move it.

WENDELL　　*(Referring to the piles)* These are all your coupons and mailings.

LINA	So?
WENDELL	Who's cluttering who?
LINA	Half this shit is yours.
WENDELL	*(Pointing to one pile)* That pile is the things you're saving up for, it's the coupons you've been cutting out,
	(Pointing to another pile) That pile is a bunch of contest envelopes for free Florida vacations you asked me to keep,
	(Pointing to another pile) That pile is a pile of strange bills I found in your underwear drawer,
	(Realizing the frustration is over everything but the piles) Lina, I meant to move the bird upstairs, and then you came home, I'm sorry—
LINA	He's staring at me.
WENDELL	I'll go put him on the roof with the other four. He's only down here 'cause Nimo said he's sick.
LINA	There are four more of these things?
WENDELL	*(Changing the subject)* You didn't take some money off my dresser this morning, did you?
LINA	No.
WENDELL	Y'know, just to, like, get to work?
LINA	I take it from your bank account—there's a chicken in our living room.
WENDELL	Seventy five bucks was missing.

LINA	*(Knowing it was Floyd)* I don't know why you're talkin' to me.
WENDELL	I'll move him upstairs.
LINA	Please get it moved before I get home tonight.
WENDELL	*(Assuredly)* I will totally take care of this by the time you get home tonight, promise.
LINA	Where's Floyd?
WENDELL	Out botherin' somebody else for a change. *(Beat)* We should make out. While we got the chance.
LINA	What?
WENDELL	You wanna make out?
LINA	*(Not too into the idea, still focused on the ROOSTER)* You wanna?
WENDELL	I mean, when again are we gonna get the chance?
LINA	How long's he been gone? You think he's looking for work?
WENDELL	If he is, we should celebrate. By making out.
LINA	*(Referring to the ROOSTER)* He's gonna stare at us while we do it.
WENDELL	No he won't. *(Sensing HER reluctance)* You should eat your McDonald's.
LINA	No.
WENDELL	Ok.
LINA	The last thing I wanted to eat tonight was McDonald's.

WENDELL	Thought you liked McDonald's.
LINA	No, you like McDonald's. Ever since I got pregnant I'll tell you one thing: your baby doesn't like McDonald's.
WENDELLL	What?
LINA	Yeah.
WENDELL	You gotta eat somethin'. Floyd says Rosalind ate like a warthog when she was pregnant.
LINA	I don't care what that ho ate.
WENDELL	Jeese.
LINA	What I say about talkin' about her?
WENDELL	Okay.
LINA	Pumpin' out babies like a fire hose.
WENDELL	She has two kids.
LINA	Taking up with another man while Floyd's at work. Don't get married if you don't want to get married, but don't bring home another man.
WENDELL	He cheated on her forever.
LINA	There is something wrong with women who do that. What if I did that to you? Took up with another man just 'cause you couldn't afford to pay the bills?
WENDELL	I pay the bills.
LINA	And what if you couldn't?
WENDELL	And you brought a man home?
LINA	Yeah. You'd call me a ho.
WENDELL	No I wouldn't.

LINA	And how does he NOT know that that oldest child is not his?
WENDELL	You gotta shut up with this.
LINA	I think he knows, he just doesn't give a shit. I mean c'mon. Theo—asthma, practically retarded—of course that's Floyd's kid, but Michael? I mean, c'mon.
WENDELL	Shut up.
LINA	Don't ever talk about Rosalind again in this house.
WENDELL	Fine. Then quiet about the kids.
LINA	Do not. Talk. About her.
WENDELL	Ok.

(WENDELL visibly sour, burps, a result of devouring his last meal too fast. HE bangs his chest to regulate HIS misbehaving chest cavity; it looks uncomfortable)

LINA	You all right?
WENDELL	Yeah. Just ate too fast.
LINA	*(Curious)* You ate already?
WENDELL	Yeah.
LINA	*(Concerned)* Wendell?
WENDELL	What?
LINA	Nothin'.
WENDELL	What?
LINA	*(Trying to put this delicately, regarding Wendell)* Were you a… healthy baby?
WENDELL	Why?
LINA	You weren't, were you?

WENDELL   My mom was fat and then she died. She forgot to mention it on the way to foster care.

LINA   I'm only asking. Wendell. It's just. I'm older.

WENDELL   I know. Eat some food. You're gonna be fine. You look great. *(Beat)* This thing's gonna make us money.

LINA   *(Admiring the rooster)* I never knew you could cut a rooster's feathers like that.

WENDELL   It's supposed to scare the other bird, when they fight.

LINA   Oh. *(Beat)* I think I need to go to the bathroom.

(LINA exits into the bathroom. WENDELL examines the ROOSTER for a moment, unsure)

WENDELL   *(To the ROOSTER)* For what's it's worth, rooster. At least everyone agrees you're a good-lookin' bird.

(WENDELL crosses to the table and takes out a McDonald's burger from the bag. HE takes a bite)

WENDELL   *(Still to the ROOSTER)* Thank God McDonald's still knows what they're doing. We may be all fucked up, guns and violence and bombs, but at least we can count on Mickey D's. Bullshit my kid doesn't like this food.

*(The sound of keys in the door lock. The door opens. **FLOYD** enters, carrying shopping bags)*

FLOYD You eatin' again?
WENDELL Shut up.
FLOYD Somebody smokin' in here?
WENDELL No.

*(**FLOYD** crosses to the bathroom door and opens it. Behind the door, **LINA**—not going to the bathroom—is smoking a cigarette)*

FLOYD Why you sittin' on the toilet?
WENDELL Lina.
LINA What?
WENDELL What are you doing?
LINA Smoking.
WENDELL Jesus.
LINA What?
WENDELL You're pregnant.
LINA People in Ireland do it all the time.
WENDELL Camilla tell you that too?
LINA Yeah.
WENDELL What I tell you about taking advice from the Irish?
LINA She's half Irish.
FLOYD Lina. What you're doing. That's not good.

WENDELL	If you didn't want the baby. You just had to tell me.
LINA	Maybe. I am.
WENDELL	*(Gathering himself)* Gimme one a those cigarettes.
LINA	*(Concerned by this)* I don't think you should.
WENDELL	You're tellin' me how I should live? Gimme one.
LINA	*(Handing **WENDELL** the entire pack)* You can have the whole pack. I have a whole carton in the closet. I had a coupon. *(Beat)* You worked so hard to quit.
WENDELL	*(To **FLOYD**, lighting up a cigarette)* What do you got in that bag?
FLOYD	Groceries.
WENDELL	Excuse me?
FLOYD	Groceries.
WENDELL	Where'd you get money to buy groceries?
FLOYD	America's economy is pickin' up.
WENDELL	Yeah. Pickin' up off my dresser.
FLOYD	I thought you left it for me.
WENDELL	What else could you possibly need? I buy you beer. We buy you food. You're a grown man and you get a stipend. What is wrong with you, taking shit from me?
FLOYD	I bought shit for the bird.
WENDELL	*(Surprised and pleased)* What?
FLOYD	Rooster supplies.
WENDELL	Really?

FLOYD	Yeah.
WENDELL	Lemme see.
FLOYD	Lina. Get off the toilet seat lid and come join us. I bought shit.
LINA	I'm fine here.

(FLOYD studies LINA)

FLOYD	Lina.
LINA	What.
FLOYD	Lina. I gotta say.
LINA	What, Floyd. What do you gotta to say.
FLOYD	I gotta say, despite you sittin' on the toilet and your crappy dress and your hair. And your pregnancy.
LINA	What?
FLOYD	I think. You look very beautiful today.
WENDELL	Excuse me?
FLOYD	Very very beautiful. You are. Today.
LINA	*(Flustered but not unflattered)* Well, thank you, Floyd.
WENDELL	Floyd. I'm standin' right here. That's my wife.
FLOYD	*(To **WENDELL**)* I know. It's just she looks very attractive. I mean, the dress could use some tailoring. But I always thought she was really pretty.
WENDELL	What the fuck is the matter with you?

LINA I gotta get ready for work now. *(To FLOYD)* Thank you Floyd. For the compliment.

(LINA exits the bathroom, enters the living room, then exits into the bedroom)

FLOYD *(To LINA as she exits, referring to WENDELL)* Make this guy go work extra time at the toll booth. You shouldn't be workin'. You should just be lookin' good.

WENDELL *(To FLOYD)* What the fuck is wrong with you?

FLOYD *(To LINA, now in the other room)* I'm doing better, Lina. I am. Days ain't like they used to be anymore. I'm training this bird now. No need for you to go to work. Not after this thing starts winning. *(To WENDELL)* She shouldn't be working pregnant.

WENDELL When you write a book on relationship advice and become a famous advice columnist, then I'll take your advice.

FLOYD What? I'm feeling good. I'm not allowed to feel good?

WENDELL No. Not when you don't got a job. Not when you say shit like that to my wife. Gimme me what's left of my money back.

FLOYD I spent it all.

WENDELL Gimme it.

FLOYD I bought a lotta shit.

(FLOYD takes out a jar of pickles from the grocery bag)

FLOYD	Here. I bought you pickles. Trust me. Feed them to her in her time of need. 'Cause if her pregnancy is anything like Rosalind's was. Fuck. *(Beat)* I called my dad up.
WENDELL	What?
FLOYD	Yeah. Long distance on your phone. While you were out.
WENDELL	What he say?
FLOYD	He gave me some recipes. To condition the cock.
WENDELL	That's great.
FLOYD	*(Taking out a slip of paper)* His voice was very irritating. Took him like a half-an-hour to spit this out. I'm glad he has trouble talkin' now.

(FLOYD hands WENDELL the recipe)

WENDELL	This is fantastic.
FLOYD	That's the magic piece of paper. It's a little different from the one we used as kids. I think.
WENDELL	Why? Get the old one.
FLOYD	He's so protective of it. I couldn't sit on that phone anymore.

WENDELL	You got all day.
FLOYD	Geronimo and me never used old school recipes anyway.
WENDELL	I'm the one paying for all this shit, get the old one.
FLOYD	No.
WENDELL	*(Reading)* What the fuck is D-Extract?
FLOYD	Part of the recipe.
WENDELL	For what?
FLOYD	We gonna make like a solvent. It's got ingredients from the orient in it. Soya bean oil, stewed tomatoes, jockey oats. It's like a paste, we are gonna make it now. Crude protein.
WENDELL	Not now we're, not with her here.
FLOYD	This bird was your fucking idea.
WENDELL	We're waitin' till she's gone.
FLOYD	When she's gone *(Removing medical tubing from the bag)* we'll teach Calagay to jump rope, run fast, keep his head back away from claws, get used to blades on his left talons, 'cause Christ knows its too late to dub him, he'll never heal in time.
WENDELL	Dub him?
FLOYD	Cut the waddle and comb.
WENDELL	What the fuck is a waddle and comb?
FLOYD	The extra crap around his face, the skin. I mean grooming, grooming is like an afterthought at this point. We're gonna

	discover the truth about how hard Geronimo conned you.
WENDELL	Floyd.
FLOYD	What?
WENDELL	Don't ever take money off my dresser again.
FLOYD	I'll do whatever the fuck I want.
WENDELL	No you won't.
FLOYD	Don't talk down to me.
WENDELL	What the hell is the matter with you?
FLOYD	Comin' in here with a rooster, telling me what I gotta do. You'd a been dead if it wasn't for me. You owe me a lot more than just seventy five dollars. I'll take shit off your dresser whenever I want.
WENDELL	I repaid you plenty.
FLOYD	Wendell. There is no amount of money in the world that could repay me for the amount of beating and raping I saved you from in that boy's home. Do you know why you're able to put together a normal life in your adulthood? Because of me. Your life is better now because I allowed it to become better by using my brain to keep us both safe. And sacrificing for you. Because I love you. I'm one who said you should go for Lina. You take her away from everybody, don't think Rosalind's not pissed they don't talk anymore. You never could get laid before without my

help and now you're on Easy Street. Because I love you and I use my mind to help you. And now I'm gonna try to use that same mind to win us tens of thousands of dollars. With five crappy ass birds. All of which are your idea. But even then it'll be me who did it, who kept us safe, and protected everything. 'Cause I know how much money you got in the can. About zero, and don't think I don't know about how Lina don't know about how little money you have. Don't talk to me about seventy five dollars again. That is just a spec on a cosmic chart of an infinite set of owing that you owe me. Don't ever embarrass me in front of your wife again.
(Beat)
Now, once Lina goes to work. I expect you to be quiet and respectful while we put this shit together. You want a fighting bird, I'll give you a fighting bird. You just gotta get outta my way.

WENDELL   Fine. As soon as Geronimo leaves.
FLOYD   What?
WENDELL   He's coming over.
FLOYD   No. Call him up. Tell him he's not welcome. I got enough weak people in my life.
WENDELL   This is my house.
FLOYD   And it's mine too until I'm gone.

SCENE 3

Setting: Early evening, about an hour later. The apartment.

*At rise, **FLOYD** standing with **GERONIMO**, a Filipino man in a mechanic's uniform. **WENDELL** is sitting. All three examine the bird, which looks a little sicker than before. On the kitchen counter sits a brown lunch bag containing something substantial.*

GERONIMO	Calagay?
WENDELL	Yeah.
GERONIMO	Wendell: Calagary.
WENDELL	What?
GERONIMO	Calagary. Canada.
FLOYD	Canada?
GERONIMO	Why did you think he was from France?
WENDELL	'Cause that's what you told me.
GERONIMO	No. I told you France is very sophisticated. I told you it would be nice to have a bird from the famous cock fighting town of Calagay, France. But this bird is from Calagary, Canada.
FLOYD	*(Correcting **GERONIMO**)* Calgary. Fucking Calgary. Say it.
GERONIMO	Calgary.
FLOYD	How hard was that?
GERONIMO	*(Serious)* Floyd. I am going to say something to both you two gentlemen: these birds are perhaps the greatest gift

	you will ever receive from anybody. If you do not win, you will probably not win anything ever again in your whole lives.
FLOYD	*(To GERONIMO)* I checked on his jumping ability and his agility and he didn't do shit, he is slow as concrete. You're not a very good breeder anymore, Nimo. Have you chorded him even? Have you even tried to harden him?
GERONIMO	Sort of.
FLOYD	What about his brothers?
GERONIMO	Sort of.
FLOYD	At least his eyes are clean. He flips okay, but I doubt he can be properly pointed in time, we gotta hope he's got instinct. He ever sparred?
GERONIMO	No.
FLOYD	Fuck. Of course not. You haven't been the same since your wife died.
GERONIMO	Fuck you.
FLOYD	Leave.
GERONIMO	Floyd. God is looking down on you. He is judging your ability to be of any value to anybody. He is asking you why you do not have a job. He is asking why you are terrible father. He is asking why he brought you into this world. God is wondering this Floyd.
FLOYD	*(To WENDELL)* Get him outta here.
WENDELL	No.

GERONIMO But at least you cut his feathers well.
WENDELL Floyd always cuts feathers well.
GERONIMO *(Perhaps referring to the bowl on the counter)* But this paste you made, this paste was a bad idea.
FLOYD *(To **WENDELL**)* Get him outta here.
WENDELL No. He bred them. He built them. He's the only one with a minivan.
FLOYD *(Turning HIS attention towards **GERONIMO**)* Nimo. If these birds are the best then why did one of his brothers die?
GERONIMO *(Beat)* What?
FLOYD Yeah. One of his brothers died.
GERONIMO When?
FLOYD Just before you got here.
WENDELL I found him on the roof. I gave him a little impromptu burial, put him in a brown paper lunch bag. *(Pointing to the BROWN PAPER BAG)* That's him over there.
FLOYD Your birds can't even survive on a rooftop in regular weather.
GERONIMO Motherfucker.
WENDELL We are gonna need another one of his brothers from his tire shop.
FLOYD Tell me you got a backup brother. *(Beat)* Tell me you bred a couple more than just five, right?
GERONIMO Of course I did.
FLOYD Well that's good.

GERONIMO Floyd.
FLOYD What?
GERONIMO Tell me you still have your knives. Every other blade we had broke at the last fight. *(Taking a blade out of his pocket and placing it on the table)* I only have one Mexican short knife left.
FLOYD So?
GERONIMO Tell me you still have your knives. *(Beat)* Floyd.
FLOYD What?
GERONIMO Where is your set of bird knives?
FLOYD *(Crossing to the table, picking up the Mexican short knife)* I sold them. I don't have them.
GERONIMO Oh boy. Ok.
FLOYD Maybe you should think twice before cutting back on your workforce.
GERONIMO You never came to work. How could you be considered part of my workforce?
FLOYD Bet you could sure use my knives now.
GERONIMO You have to sweet talk to your father. We need his Cubano knives. We need his recipe.
FLOYD Fuck you.
GERONIMO Your father is going to be dead soon anyway.
FLOYD So?
GERONIMO He is probably going to leave them to you. Just get them early.

FLOYD	He's not going to leave them to me.
WENDELL	Nimo, don't talk about his dad being dead.
GERONIMO	Floyd. One more time, let's do this thing, I raise, you train, we win a lot of money. You can move out. Wendell doesn't have to give Rosalind money for the children. We are all happy.

(Beat)

FLOYD	What?
WENDELL	Nimo.
FLOYD	*(Stunned)* What?
GERONIMO	*(To FLOYD)* Give this poor guy a break. Let's win money for him.
FLOYD	*(To WENDELL)* When you do that?
WENDELL	*(To GERONIMO)* Why'd you say that?
FLOYD	*(To WENDELL)* When you do that?
WENDELL	*(To FLOYD)* When didn't I do that?
FLOYD	She doesn't need money.
GERONIMO	*(Sarcastic)* Ok, she doesn't.
WENDELL	What the fuck did you think was going on? You thought you were paying all your bills selling roosters and patching tires for a living? Rosalind can't hold a steady job. I just thought you were just too embarrassed to say anything.
FLOYD	*(To WENDELL)* You really been doin' that?

WENDELL Floyd, of course I have. What else am I supposed to do?

GERONIMO Go see your father.

FLOYD Shut up. *(Beat, to **WENDELL**)* You really been doin' that?

WENDELL Floyd. She was in a really bad place for a while.

GERONIMO *(Focused)* Floyd. Honestly. I could give a shit about your kids. Get your father's recipe. Take my minivan. Get the morning-of recipe, then get his knives. Then fuck him in the face for me.

FLOYD *(Touched?)* You really wanna lend me your minivan?

GERONIMO Yes.

FLOYD Ok.

GERONIMO I suppose you are going to need the money for the tolls too?

WENDELL It's like twenty five bucks for tolls.

FLOYD *(Exploding, totally crazy)* I don't ever wanna hear about you motherfuckers ever giving Rosalind money again. *(To **GERONIMO**)* Yes I need twenty five dollars. Yes I need your keys. I'm gonna drive up there tonight, I'm gonna fuckin' camp out, and I'll take that fucker to the dog track first thing. 'Cause this is gonna take work. This is gonna take convincing. You want a recipe, I'll give you a recipe. You want knives, I'll get you knives.

30

	Don't ever give Rosalind money again. Give me the keys.
GERONIMO	*(Giving **FLOYD** the keys)* Here.
FLOYD	*(Taking them)* Now give me the twenty five bucks.

SCENE 4

SCENE: Late that night. The apartment.

*At rise, the television is on to a talk show, of the self-help variety. **LINA** is seated on the La-Z-Boy. Still in HER work attire, SHE is opening mail. A beer sits unopened nearby. SHE takes a cigarette out of a pack and lights it, then regards the ROOSTER.*

LINA *(To the ROOSTER)* You don't mind if I smoke, do you bird?

(SHE takes a big drag. SHE opens another piece of mail)

LINA *(To the ROOSTER, referring to the opened piece of mail)* Oh look, we won another car. *(Beat)* I'd give away Mazdas too if I had them.

(SHE takes another drag, then opens more mail. SHE reads)

31

LINA *(With a distant ennui)* Why didn't we pay this? *(Lifting up another envelope, perhaps holding it up to the light to see its contents, but not about to open it, then perhaps to the ROOSTER)* If that last statement made me sad, this Visa bill's gonna make me suicidal

(Then prompted by subject matter being talked about on the television)

You married bird? "Do you still love your spouse?"

(SHE puts the envelope down, then opens the can of beer, taking a sip. SHE stares at the ROOSTER, perhaps guiltily)

LINA *(Defensively, to the ROOSTER)* People in Ireland do it all the time.

SCENE 5

Setting: The next day. The stadium-style seats at the greyhound track in Bridgeport, CT.

*At rise, **FLOYD** sitting with his dad, **FELIX**, who is old and suffering from a condition; the left half of his body does not respond well and his speech is slurred. As much as possible,*

FELIX's responses come from nodding and motioning, but HE cannot resist the urge to speak.

FELIX   He.
FLOYD   He what? What did he do?
FELIX   He.
FLOYD   C'mon Broken Brain. Formulate a new sentence, I know you got another thought in there, fight through this, what'd the nurse say.
FELIX   He. Called. Me.
FLOYD   You didn't have to answer.
FELIX   *(Again, not wanting to say it again, trying to say something else)* He. Called. Me.
FLOYD   I know. You told me.
FELIX   *(One more time, then embarrassed)* He.
FLOYD   He what? Jesus.
FELIX   He's. A good kid. Wendell.
FLOYD   He is, huh?
FELIX   Wendell's. A. Good. Kid.
FLOYD   Then what am I?
FELIX   You. Are. A. Good kid too.
FLOYD   Even though you got mush mouth I can still tell you lie.

(Pause)

FELIX   Where. Is. Geronimo?

FLOYD Playing with used Goodyear radials in the Boogie Down Bronx like a child, what do you care?

FELIX *(Clearly trying to ask something else)* Wendell. Called. Me.

FLOYD You're, like, trapped in there, aren't you? You were talkin' about something else, and now you're, just, back to the old thought.

FELIX I. Am. Learning. Wendell called me. *(Believing that HE is saying a new thought, but only realizing after HE has not)* Wendell. Is. A. Good. Kid.

FLOYD Start over. When that happens, start over. You were right there when the nurse said it. Do what she says or repeat like a recording your whole life. You were smart enough to desert me to cut down on expenses so you gotta be smart enough to try and start to talk normally for five seconds.

(FELIX returns to his dog racing magazine, after a moment HE tries to speak again)

FELIX I. Hate. This.
FLOYD Well I hate you, so imagine how I feel.
FELIX Please. Be nice.
FLOYD Ok. I'm sorry. *(Beat)* That recipe you gave me sucked. It made the bird sicker.

	(Trying to be nice) What, what do you hate?
FELIX	What?
FLOYD	You said you "hate this," what do you hate?
FELIX	This.
FLOYD	The dog track, the fact that it's gonna rain, the fact you gotta beg Wendell and me for money when we barely got any, or the fact you got a stroke? Which one do you hate?
FELIX	*(Referring to his condition)* This.
FLOYD	Well I'm sorry about it. I'm sure its very frustrating.
FELIX	Thank-you. For. Coming.
FLOYD	No problem. Nimo lent me his car. It was no problem.
FELIX	Geronimo. Geronimo. (Starting over) Is. A. Nice guy.
FLOYD	Yeah, for a flip he's a real nice guy.
FELIX	He. He. *(Focusing)* Geronimo. Is. A nice guy.
FLOYD	This is a real boring conversation.
FELIX	He. Is. Filipino.
FLOYD	Yup. That's true. And he doesn't like you very much anymore. Look, *(Handing **FELIX** a pad and paper)* give us the regimen. We could have some good birds here. One of them died, I brought him for you to take a look. But I still think they

	might be good, maybe later you can show me how you used to fasten the Mexican short knife, he's still got it on. *(Referring the DEAD ROOSTER, perhaps showing the knife strapped to the talon)* Please. For us. Give us the ingredients.
FELIX	You. You. Make it right?
FLOYD	What?
FELIX	The. The. Recipe. I gave you.
FLOYD	Pop. Course I did.
FELIX	No. No. I-bet-no.
FLOYD	I made what you told me to make.
FELIX	I bet. You made. It wrong.
FLOYD	Why? Why do you think that?
FELIX	How. How. How did you like. My nurse?
FLOYD	What?
FELIX	My nurse.
FLOYD	That nurse of yours is totally hot.
FELIX	She is totally. Hot. She, though. Is mean.
FLOYD	I'm gonna let you in on a secret: They're gonna keep on peeling away priveliges at that home, first they'll be mean, then lights out at nine, then no TV, then no butter, then you die.
FELIX	*(Referring to the six-pack at **FLOYD**'s feet)* Will. My. Medication?
FLOYD	What?
FELIX	Allow-me. To. To have a beer?
FLOYD	I don't know. Might be dangerous.
FELIX	Can. I. Have. A beer?

FLOYD   No.
FELIX   Why? Why not?
FLOYD   Captain Blood Clot, what's the magic word?
FELIX   *(Beat)* Please.
FLOYD   There.
FELIX   (Working hard) Please. Can-I. Have. A beer?
FLOYD   No.

(FELIX returns to his dog racing paper. FLOYD hands a beer to him. FELIX stares at him helplessly)

FELIX   Please. Open. Bottle.
FLOYD   Ok.

(FLOYD does nothing)

FELIX   Please.

(FLOYD opens the beer and hands the beer to FELIX. FELIX tries hard to take a sip but dribbles on himself)

FLOYD   If you're gonna dribble on yourself, you should use a straw.
FELIX   You have. One?
FLOYD   *(Removing a straw from the bag)* Yes, I have one, I grabbed one from the package store. *(Beat)* Why do they call them package stores up here?

FELIX	No.
FLOYD	I hate this state.
FELIX	No. I don't. Want a. Straw.
FLOYD	You sure?

(FELIX nods)

FLOYD	Suit yourself, Dribble Monster.
FELIX	How. How. Is. Rosalind?
FLOYD	She's a slut. I moved out.
FELIX	She is. She is nice.
FLOYD	No, she's not.
FELIX	How. Is. Theo?
FLOYD	Fine. He's got Asthma now, but it's always something with him.
FELIX	Theo doesn't. Theo doesn't—
FLOYD	What?
FELIX	Visit.
FLOYD	He's five.
FELIX	Michael visits.
FLOYD	Stop making up shit.
FELIX	Michael. Visits. He visited.
FLOYD	When?
FELIX	He has. A junior high. Dance. Next week.
FLOYD	He visited? Here?
FELIX	Port Authority. He. Wanted. To talk.
FLOYD	Why?
FELIX	He. Is. A-good-kid.
FLOYD	He's gotten a little too chubby and a little too swishy for me.

FELIX No.

FLOYD Where the fuck he learn to take a bus?

FELIX He is like you. When. When you were young. Travelling.

FLOYD He wasn't put in an orphanage by a father who was too busy to care for him. So we're a little different like that.

(FELIX drinks and dribbles on himself, as prophesied)

FLOYD Now that you've had your bath, *(Indicating the pen and paper)* Write down the real recipe we used for roosters, before the race starts. Don't you dare fuck with me. Pretend like you're writing out your will.

FELIX Steroids?

FLOYD What?

FELIX Do. You. Want? Steriods?

FLOYD Why would I want steroids?

FELIX Recipes. With steroids. They-have. Steroid recipes. Now for birds.

FLOYD Did we give birds steroids when I was young?

(FELIX shakes his head no)

FLOYD Did we win when I was young?
(FELIX shakes his head yes)

FLOYD Then why would I want steroids? Last thing I want is a more bulky bird.
FELIX You-buy-them-at-the-vitamin-stores.
FLOYD Even in that *(Referring to **FELIX**'s mind)* lock box of a brain. You're still fuckin' with me.
FELIX Mormons. Invented. Bird steroids.
FLOYD Stop it. Dad.
FELIX Mormons. Are into / roosters.
FLOYD Stop / it.
FELIX In Utah, Mormons in Utah—

*(**FLOYD** hits **FELIX** hard)*

FLOYD You made me do that. You are not allowed to do that to me anymore. Write down the recipe, write down the old way. What we did when I was a kid.

*(Fearing another strike, **FELIX** begins to write furiously)*

FELIX *(Trying not to say this)* Mormons—
FLOYD STOP REPEATING THE THING YOU JUST GOT HIT FOR!
FELIX *(Focusing)* Please-don't. Hit me.
FLOYD Ok. I won't hit you. *(Beat)* I'm sorry I hit you.
FELIX Ok. Ok.

(FELIX cowers, and stops writing. The starting bell of the gates opening sound, the race has begun, FELIX pays attention although in pain)

FLOYD Who'd you bet on?
FELIX *(Starting over)* I don't. Bet anymore. Watching. Is fine.
FLOYD Watching doesn't sound like you.
FELIX I. I like watching. I will-be. Adopting a dog.
FLOYD You're going to be adopting a dog? Like a greyhound? Where you gonna put it?
FELIX In. My house.
FLOYD House?
FELIX When I move. Out of. The center. When-I-get-better.
FLOYD *(Now curious)* When are you getting better?
FELIX I will adopt. Even if. I don't. Get. Better. I will feed him. In the back yard. Of-the-center.
FLOYD They're not going to let you do that.
FELIX They. Might.
FLOYD Want some rum?
FELIX Yes.
FLOYD Then finish writing.
FELIX Don't. Hit me.
FLOYD Ok.

(FELIX writes, then stops)

FELIX   I. Am. Done.
FLOYD   *(Handing **FELIX** another beer)* Here. Congrats. Have some rum, Drunken Master.

(**FLOYD** opens it for **FELIX**)

FELIX   Thank. Thank you.
FLOYD   No problem.

*(**FELIX** drinks it really fast, dribbling some, but getting most of it down)*

FLOYD   *(Referring to the race)* Which one you pick to win?
FELIX   Five. Five.
FLOYD   *(Looking out, noticing the dog is ahead)* Five is going to win.
FELIX   I know. That's why. I think. He will win.

(Number Five wins)

FELIX   See?
FLOYD   Yeah.

*(**FELIX**, it appears, is beginning to slump from the alcohol consumption)*

FELIX   This rum. Tastes good.

FLOYD   Well I guess that's good then. You dirty Cuban. Gimme the recipe.

(FLOYD grabs the recipe from FELIX, opens himself a beer as if in celebration, then reads the slip of paper. After a moment, it becomes apparent that what is on the sheet of paper is seriously troubling to FLOYD)

FLOYD   Why would you write something like this?

(FELIX has very grown very nearly unconscious, perhaps blubbering a bit. Furious at the information on the note, FLOYD takes out one of the last beers from the bag and pours it down FELIX's limp throat. HE throws the bottle to the ground, reaches into FELIX's pockets, and takes out HIS wallet and removes HIS cash, ID's, and photographs. Beat: FLOYD catches a glimpse of one of the photographs)

FLOYD   Only you would have a photograph of a fucking greyhound and not one of your son. You pig. *(Taking the DEAD ROOSTER—perhaps still in the bag—and throwing it in FELIX's lap)* Take this fuckin' rooster, hope the Connecticut cops shove the Mexican short knife up your ass. All I needed was your fuckin' advice. *(Perhaps hitting FELIX hard with the DEAD ROOSTER)* Fuck you. And fuck your greyhound.

SCENE 6

Setting: Late that night. The apartment.

*At rise, **LINA** is sipping on a can of beer. HER cigarettes and lighter are in plain view. A knock is heard at the door. **LINA** takes a big swig from her beer and then throws it in the garbage. Another knock. **LINA** crosses to the door and presses her ear against the frame.*

LINA	Yes?
ROSALIND	*(OS)* Lina. I need to ask you a question.
LINA	Who is this?
ROSALIND	*(OS)* Who the fuck else would knock on your door at eleven at night?
LINA	Go away.
ROSALIND	*(OS)* Lina, c'mon
LINA	Rosalind. Go away.
ROSALIND	*(OS)* No. I'm just gonna keep on knockin'.

*(**ROSALIND** knocks three times, forcefully)*

LINA	I thought ho's only walked the street.
ROSALIND	*(OS)* Say something like that to my face with the door open. *(Beat)* Can I talk to your husband?
LINA	Wendell's sleeping. If I let you in, by the time you take off your coat you'll have fucked him.

44

ROSALIND *(OS) (Truly nice)* Please. Angel, c'mon. Let me in.
LINA *(Quietly)* No.
ROSALIND *(OS)* Please. *(Beat)* Lina. It's just me.

(LINA undoes the deadbolt and opens the door. Rosalind stands at the door, disheveled)

LINA Make one fucking eye at Wendell while you're here and I'll stab your eye with scissors.
ROSALIND Thank you for letting me in.
LINA You look like shit girl.
ROSALIND *(Referring to the bedroom)* He sleeping in there?
LINA What did I just say about talking about my husband?
ROSALIND *(Meaning it)* Sorry.
LINA Why do you always want somebody else's things?
ROSALIND Lina, I don't want your husband.
LINA I don't see you for months, and now you're showing up here out of the blue at midnight? What else could you possibly want?
ROSALIND Honey, when did you develop this whole paranoia thing?
LINA When did you develop this whole I'm busted thing?
ROSALIND Could you try and be nice?

*(A beat as **LINA** considers this. **ROSALIND** settles in, perhaps taking a seat. SHE notices the ROOSTER)*

ROSALIND   You got a. You got a bird in the house.
LINA   Get outta here.
ROSALIND   That's a big bird. This is an apartment building. You know that, right?
LINA   Leave.
ROSALIND   (Recalling) Wait, oh shit, that, is that Nimo's bird?
LINA   You heard about it?
ROSALIND   Yeah. Why's it in your apartment?
LINA   It's sick. You really heard about it?
ROSALIND   Wow. That looks impressive.
LINA   You think so?
ROSALIND   Totally. You think it could win?
LINA   I don't know.
ROSALIND   Who gets the money if it does?
LINA   Why don't you try getting a job?
ROSALIND   That thing looks like it could kick some ass.
LINA   Rosalind.
ROSALIND   What?
LINA   What do you want?
ROSALIND   I need to talk to Wendell.
LINA   What do you got to talk to him about?
ROSALIND   Things.
LINA   I already got your husband living on my couch 'cause you couldn't keep your legs

	shut, you don't get to talk to Wendell about things.
ROSALIND	The dude was rich. Floyd does shit like this constantly. Tired a people callin' me a slut all the time.
LINA	Well then what would you like to be called?
ROSALIND	Practical. *(Beat)* Eat some pickles. You're pregnant. You're emotional. How 'bout offering me something to drink?
LINA	We don't keep drinks in this house.
ROSALIND	In this house? Excuse me? Did I get lost in the hallway?
LINA	Rosalind, I'm tired, I just got home from work. Could you please leave?
ROSALIND	Lina?
LINA	What?
ROSALIND	Wendell was supposed to lend me some money.
LINA	Lend you money?
ROSALIND	This is hard enough. Don't make it harder.
LINA	Lend you money for what? We don't have any money.
ROSALIND	Can't believe you have a rooster in your house.
LINA	Don't change the subject.
ROSALIND	Michael's got his junior high dance thing coming up. And Theodore, with the asthma.
LINA	So?

ROSALIND *(Looking around the apartment more, noticing the contest envelopes)*
What's with the contest envelopes? You win something recently?

LINA No.

ROSALIND You ever open up the paper and read about somebody who actually won those things?

LINA *(Snapping)* Why would Wendell give you money?

ROSALIND I don't know, I just need some now, can you give me some? He's been doing it for years.

LINA Years?

ROSALIND Yeah, but since your belly started getting bigger, things have kind of dried up. Can I have that drink now? I'd even have some of that Black Velvet shit.

LINA We don't keep liquor in this house.

ROSALIND Give me one of my fuckin' husband's beers. I'm sure there's plenty in the fridge.

LINA You're disgusting.

ROSALIND I'm disgusting? You got a barnyard animal in your living room. You should start doing normal human stuff again. Like comin' out with the girls once in a while again.

LINA Look what hanging out with you resulted in.

ROSALIND   It resulted in what used to be two really good friends.

(LINA opens the refrigerator. Several six packs of beer are visibly on display. In fact, besides the pickles and bird ingredients, nothing much else is in there. SHE grabs a beer and brings one to ROSALIND, who opens it and takes a sip)

ROSALIND   Thank you. *(Beat)* How's your dirty friend Camilla?
LINA   She's not dirty.
ROSALIND   Sure she's not. She still work at the same motherfuckin' counter?
LINA   She works at a different counter now from when you worked there.
ROSALIND   *(Offers LINA some of her beer)* Here. You should have one of this. Looks like you need it.
LINA   Rosalind, I'm pregnant.
ROSALIND   So was I, honey, so was I.
LINA   No, I don't do that.
ROSALIND   Think of it like this: you're giving baby a break from her day-to-day. It's like a vacation for your baby. I don't care what the doctor's say. *(Noticing the inexpensive cigarettes on the table)* Shit, Lina, you're smokin' those now?
LINA   They're Wendell's.
ROSALIND   What, you have a coupon?
LINA   Yeah.

ROSALIND Coupons. Jesus.
LINA *(Beat)* Michael's got a dance?
ROSALIND Yeah. This whole "dance prom thing," it's kind of gay in this day and age, isn't it?
LINA No.
ROSALIND They get all dressed up, it's pretty gay.
LINA Getting dressed up is kind of nice.
ROSALIND Well, if you do it like Michael does it's gay. *(Beat)* Caught him in my bedroom the other day with that Indian kid.
LINA Ravinder?
ROSALIND Yeah. You know him? His parents got those blue turbans?
LINA Little Ravinder?
ROSALIND Little? He ain't little. No wonder Michael brought him home. Ravinder was so scared I was going to tell his Sikh parents.
LINA Ravinder. Really?
ROSALIND So much for Michael being young for his grade. *(Suddenly serious)* Lina.
LINA What?
ROSALIND You gotta promise not to say anything to Floyd. Last thing that kid needs is Floyd telling him he's a mutant.
LINA I swear. I won't. I promise.
ROSALIND Ravinder's father would beat the crap outta him. Who knows what they keep in those turbans.
LINA Lemme have a sip of your beer.
ROSALIND What?

LINA   Can I have a sip of your beer?
ROSALIND   Honey, it's your beer.

(LINA takes the can from Rosalind and takes a substantial sip)

LINA   That tastes good.
ROSALIND   Drinking with a baby sometimes is the only way to go. Makes your titties stop hurting for a minute.
LINA   Rosalind.
ROSALIND   What?
LINA   I don't want to have this baby.
ROSALIND   You don't know what you're saying. All you gotta do is birth it—
LINA   Birth is gonna hurt—
ROSALIND   The rest will take care of itself. Drink your beer.

(LINA takes a substantial drink from the beer)

ROSALIND   Damn, honey.
LINA   I'm a little drunk.
ROSALIND   Floyd convinced you to put this bird in here, didn't he?
LINA   Wendell brought it home.
ROSALIND   Doesn't seem like a Wendell thing.

*(The sound of **WENDELL** stirring in the bedroom can be heard)*

LINA   He's awake. He's gonna come to the refrigerator.

(WENDELL enters groggily and heads to the refrigerator. HE has obviously just thrown on a pair of jeans for the trip)

WENDELL Who you talking to?
LINA Nobody.
ROSALIND Hi Wendell.
LINA Rosalind.
WENDELL Rosalind?
ROSALIND How you doing, baby?
WENDELL What the fuck you doing here?
LINA She came to borrow some money Wendell. You know anything about that?
WENDELL *(To ROSALIND)* What I tell you about mentioning that to people.
ROSALIND I didn't mention it to people. Until it stopped coming.
LINA She says you been doing this since for years. That's a long time, honey. You never told me this when we got married.
WENDELL You know what, Lina? I don't feel like I got an obligation to explain everything to everybody all the time. Especially not after midnight.
LINA Wendell.
WENDELL *(Snapping, cranky from being woken up)* I pay most of the bills around here! What's

	wrong with me doin' something that I thought was right?
LINA	Are you tryin' to tell me something?
WENDELL	If I told you you woulda made me stop doin' it, calling her a slut all the time.
ROSALIND	Then why'd you stop doing it?
WENDELL	Have you seen my wife's belly? Have you noticed your husband doesn't come home to you anymore? Have you noticed the male chicken in my living room?
ROSALIND	You're like a big yeti in the morning.
WENDELL	It's not the morning! It's fucking midnight— *(To LINA, noticing the beer)* Were you drinking a beer?
LINA	I had a half a one.
ROSALIND	Or eighty percent, but whatever.
WENDELL	*(To LINA)* What the fuck is wrong with my life? Trying to do things right is, like, fucking useless. You said you wouldn't drink.
ROSALIND	Wendell, when you're upset, you're really really cute.
LINA	Fuck you Rosalind.
ROSALIND	*(To LINA)* No. Fuck you. Don't talk to me like that. You got a good man and you're always treatin' him like shit. Ungrateful bitch.

(LINA slaps ROSALIND hard)

ROSALIND *(Beat, composing HERSELF)* You're lucky you got that belly.

(ROSALIND exits into the bathroom)

WENDELL	Jesus. *(Absorbing it all, then gently)* Lina.
LINA	What?
WENDELL	*(Beat)* I need you to do me a favor.
LINA	No.
WENDELL	You're gonna go over to the stash a money that you keep in back of your closet and shove her like a hundred bucks. Just get her outta here. I need to go back to sleep.
LINA	I don't have a stash of money.
WENDELL	I see it every time I put on my slippers, yes you do.
LINA	You know about that?
WENDELL	I thought you deserved your privacy. Give her some money. Stop drinking. Give her what she wants.
LINA	What she wants? I want to go out on a Friday night, I want to not be saddled with debt like my mother, I want a decent non-fast food meal, you're the one who wants the baby. You're the one who wants a family, NO, you give her your money, I'm so sick of you making me feel bad.

(ROSALIND exits from the bathroom. Almost simultaneously, keys are heard in the door as FLOYD enters, looking rough)

ROSALIND	*(To FLOYD)* Hello Floyd.
FLOYD	*(To ROSALIND)* What the fuck are you doing here?
WENDELL	No, no, turn away and go back from where you came from, sleep in the minivan.
ROSALIND	Floyd. We were just talking about how good-looking you used to be.
FLOYD	You have a whole apartment, go home. I'm already killing these people.
ROSALIND	Maybe you should have thought of that before you were the worst father on the planet for twelve years.
FLOYD	*(To WENDELL)* Get her out of here.
WENDELL	No.
LINA	Floyd.
FLOYD	What?
LINA	Did you cut a bird's feathers in the bathtub?
FLOYD	Yeah. Why? That's not right?
LINA	You can't cut them on the Earth outside?
FLOYD	Next time I will.
ROSALIND	He's lying.
FLOYD	SHUT UP.
ROSALIND	NO.
FLOYD	*(To WENDELL, handing him a slip of paper)* Look what my dad wrote.

(WENDELL takes the piece of paper and reads)

FLOYD	*(To **ROSALIND**)* You know Michael's been to visit my dad?
ROSALIND	Yes.
WENDELL	*(Referring to the note)* He wrote this?
FLOYD	*(To **ROSALIND**)* Maybe you shoulda told me he was visiting him?
ROSALIND	What's this sudden concern for your kids?
WENDELL	Michael visited Felix?
FLOYD	*(To **WENDELL**)* You believe that?
ROSALIND	He deserves to do what he wants.
WENDELL	He's twelve years old. What he do, take a bus?
ROSALIND	Somebody's gotta visit him.
FLOYD	What kind of mother are you?
ROSALIND	It drops him off right there.
WENDELL	*(Reading the note, disbelief)* What the fuck is this? He really wrote this?
FLOYD	You know anything about that Wendell?
WENDELL	Jesus Christ.
LINA	What?
FLOYD	You gotta read this Lina, it is very interesting.

*(LINA crosses to **WENDELL** and reads the slip of paper)*

ROSALIND	Lemme see.

(ROSALIND grabs the note and reads it)

FLOYD	*(To **ROSALIND**)* What's that all about? Something you want to tell me?
ROSALIND	Floyd, you know that notes not true.
WENDELL	*(Discovering a wallet amidst **FLOYD**'s possessions on the counter)* What's this?
FLOYD	I had to take his wallet to preserve his stuff, to keep it from dropping all over, he dribbled everywhere. You can probably see beer on the paper, it went all over.
WENDELL	*(Realising)* What's he gonna do without his wallet?
FLOYD	If I were governor of a state I'd make dog tracks illegal.
ROSALIND	Floyd.
FLOYD	What?
ROSALIND	*(Putting something together)* Why do you have his wallet?
FLOYD	I don't know. I had to take it from him.
WENDELL	*(Putting something together too)* Floyd.
FLOYD	What?
WENDELL	Why the fuck do you got Felix's wallet?
FLOYD	He should be giving us money.
WENDELL	His license in there?

(ROSALIND picks up the wallet and examines the contents)

FLOYD	Yeah so.
ROSALIND	And so are his pictures.

FLOYD	Notice not a single photo of his grandchildren.
ROSALIND	Do you have any photos of your kids in your wallet?
FLOYD	No. I'm not their grandfather. Notice the photo of the fucking greyhound he wants to buy?
ROSALIND	Please tell me you didn't do what I think you did.
LINA	What?
FLOYD	I don't know what you're talking about.
ROSALIND	Sure you do.
WENDELL	No.
LINA	What?
WENDELL	*(Now knowing)* Please tell me you didn't.
LINA	What?
WENDELL	Floyd.
ROSALIND	Jesus.
FLOYD	What?
WENDELL	You fucking grandpa dumped him?
LINA	What?
ROSALIND	Floyd.
LINA	"Grandpa dumped"?
ROSALIND	Jesus.
LINA	What's he talking about?
FLOYD	Nothing. Ignore them.
LINA	You left your dad at the track?
FLOYD	Not really.
LINA	He's in Connecticut all alone?

FLOYD It's his home. *(Referring to the wallet)* See? He's even got a Connecticut driver's license.
LINA Don't you think he might need it?
ROSALIND You're nasty.
LINA I'm going to lay down.

(LINA begins to head to the bedroom)

FLOYD You know, it's a real misnomer, "grandpa dumped." He's not my grandpa.
WENDELL He's Michael's granpa, he's Theo's granpa!
FLOYD Yeah? Is he Wendell?

(LINA enters the bedroom)

ROSALIND No wonder your boys are all fucked up.
WENDELL You're terrifying. Gimme the fucking keys to the car. What bleacher you leave him in?
FLOYD I forgot.
WENDELL Fuck you. I'm going to get the recipe.
FLOYD 100 miles away and the Bridgeport park closed at nine. I'd say tomorrow'd be the day for that.
WENDELL The cockfight's tomorrow. Hope you get fucking arrested.
FLOYD You have no idea how expensive he was.
WENDELL Expensive.
FLOYD Emotionally Expensive.

*(**WENDELL** takes the two leftover hamburgers off the plate, wraps in a paper towel, and puts them in his pocket)*

FLOYD What's that for?
WENDELL The road.
FLOYD You eat too much.
WENDELL You leave old men at the track too much.
ROSALIND Wendell, I just want to leave. Michael's got a dance.
WENDELL So?
ROSALIND Don't do this to me.
WENDELL I don't care what Michael's got. He's goin' with a boy anyway. I'm outta money. Tell Michael to get a job. He might be gay, but he's the most equipped man I know at this point. Or you could try showing up to work five days a week, but whatever. A guy I consider the closest thing I got to a father just got grandpa dumped in Bridgeport, Connecticut. And he's supposed to help me win this cockfight. No more money. No more help. All I want is a fucking recipe.
FLOYD Who is gay?
ROSALIND Nobody's, he's delusional—
WENDELL Delusional? He shimmies up and down the Grand Concourse daily like a woman to the D-Train. *(To **FLOYD**)* I've been sick since you walked in this house. I don't even have the strength to tell my wife

60

	who's having a baby to stop smoking a cigarette in the bathroom. Try not fuck anything up while I'm gone.
FLOYD	The park's closed.
WENDELL	Then I'm breaking in.
FLOYD	95's got construction everywhere.
WENDELL	Stop lying to me. *(Smelling LINA's cigarette)* Lina, stop smoking that fucking cigarette, that's my baby too! *(To FLOYD)* Give me the fucking keys.
FLOYD	Maybe you should ask Geronimo if it's okay. It's his car.

(WENDELL grabs the keys and FELIX's wallet from FLOYD and exits)

ROSALIND	*(To FLOYD)* Well, at least you're getting along with your new family.
FLOYD	Who's gay? What the fuck was he talking about?
ROSALIND	Who the fuck knows.
FLOYD	What did he mean? Do you know what he's talking about?
ROSALIND	No.
FLOYD	You better not be lying to me.
ROSALIND	Oh no. I better not be lying to you.

(Beat. THEY regard EACH OTHER)

FLOYD You look good.

ROSALIND   So do you.

(LINA enters from her bedroom with a handful of cash and crosses to ROSALIND)

LINA   Here. Use this for your boys. We don't got enough to do anything worthwhile with it anyway. Like buy diapers. So why don't you have some?

(LINA hands ROSALIND the cash)

ROSALIND	Lina.
FLOYD	My boys don't need anything.
LINA	Take it. It's the money you can't provide.
ROSALIND	Thanks Lina.
LINA	Now could you please leave?
ROSALIND	Sure.
LINA	Thank you.

(ROSALIND heads towards the door)

ROSALIND	Just in case—
LINA	What? You get off welfare?
FLOYD	Jesus Lina.

(ROSALIND exits, deeply hurt by this final insult. Pause)

FLOYD Lina. I apologize for crammin' my smells into your tiny apartment. This place is too small for three people.

LINA It's like livin' with a whole lion shitting on the floor.

FLOYD Yeah. I guess it is.

LINA I can't believe you left your father at the track.

FLOYD Try growing up with him, then without him, then with him, then you'll start to understand.

LINA No, I don't think I would.

FLOYD Well, I'm sorry about that.

LINA You're a monster.

FLOYD I know. I'm a monster.

LINA He must be terrified.

FLOYD Try being defenseless in a boy's home. That's also terrifying.

LINA That excuse is so tired.

FLOYD Bet its not too tired a topic for Wendell.

LINA Only you exploit your childhood for sympathy.

FLOYD Maybe you should give Wendell some for his.

LINA I do.

FLOYD Do you have any idea what kinda woman his mother was? She was the kinda person who takes up five seats on the subway. Blubber and wheezing. She even had whiskers. You've seen the pictures. *(Beat)*

	That said. If she hadn't a died. I woulda had nobody.
LINA	You gotta move out.
FLOYD	I will. Very very soon. *(Beat, then to the ROOSTER)* Well it looks like it's you and me, Calgary.
LINA	Calgary?
FLOYD	Yup. Calgary.
LINA	Calagay.
FLOYD	Calagay? No. Calgary.
LINA	What?
FLOYD	This bird's from Canada. Wendell misheard. Geronimo can't speak. It's from Calgary, Canada. Not France.
LINA	*(Beat)* I can't believe I'm gonna say this. It takes the romance out of it.
FLOYD	Tell me about it.
LINA	I think I'm still gonna call it Calagay.
FLOYD	I think that'll be fine. You should get into this rooster. It's a very handsome rooster.
LINA	I don't know if I can get into anything anymore.
FLOYD	No. Come here. Look at it. It looks good at night.
LINA	No. It's got like salmanilla. I'm gonna get bird flu.
FLOYD	No. Come look.

(LINA crosses to the bird)

LINA	It's so bright.
FLOYD	I know.
LINA	You did his feathers so nice.
FLOYD	I'm pretty good at that, yeah.
LINA	Your dad teach you that?
FLOYD	Yeah. *(Beat)* Lina.
LINA	What?
FLOYD	Lina. I know you been drinking a lot lately. Even before you were pregnant. You should slow down.
LINA	The bird looks nice.
FLOYD	*(Beat)* It does, doesn't it?
LINA	*(Gently)* You know that notes not true, right?
FLOYD	Whatever's true, Lina, I'd like to not think about it.

(Pause)

LINA	*(Feeling something)* Floyd, why you touchin' my leg.
FLOYD	Sorry. It was an accident.
LINA	No it wasn't.
FLOYD	Ok.
LINA	That what you used to do? With the other ladies? Even after you were married?
FLOYD	No.
LINA	You'd sneak into their houses at night. When their husbands weren't home?
FLOYD	No.

LINA	That's what you did, wasn't it? And why Rosalind would always be crying over here. To Wendell.
FLOYD	She'd cry over here?
LINA	This is how you used to do it, right?
FLOYD	*(Beat)* Yeah. Sometimes.
LINA	Floyd.
FLOYD	What.
LINA	Do it again. *(Beat)* Hurry. *(Beat)* 'Cause I got to get some sleep.

SCENE 7

Setting: About an hour-and-a-half before dawn. Stadium-style seats at the greyhound track in Bridgeport, CT.

*At rise, **WENDELL** sitting with **FELIX**, who looks as though he has had a tough night. **FELIX** is no longer sitting in the stadium seat, but instead squatting on the ground with the folding portion of the seat at his back.*

WENDELL	So you just bunkered down here below your seat? So no one would see you?
FELIX	Yes. Yes. *(Stopping himself)* They don't. Clean well, the management.
WENDELL	Obviously. Just write down the recipe. No more D-extract solvents. No more mean spirited notes. Ok, Felix?
FELIX	I have. No pen.

WENDELL	I do. *(Handing a pen and paper to **FELIX**)* 95, the whole road, I hate this fucking state, write it down. *(Noticing the bottles at **FELIX**'s feet)* Why do you got all these beer bottles you got at your feet.
FELIX	Floyd. Gave. Them. To me.
WENDELL	What kind of medication are you on?
FELIX	I. Am not. Sure.
WENDELL	How are you not sure?
FELIX	They just. Give. Them to me. *(Beat)* Floyd-knows-though. He-talked-to-my. To my. *(Having trouble)* Hot. Nurse.
WENDELL	Hot nurse?
FELIX	My hot nurse.
WENDELL	Damn. You look like hell. *(Looking around)* How did they not see you here? I saw you right away.
FELIX	I was—lying-down. Long-ways. The seats. Looked normal. No one cleans. This dog track. *(Stopping himself, HE reveals the Mexican short knife wrapped around his index finger as if it were a claw)* I put this on. In case. Of attack.
WENDELL	What the fuck is that?
FELIX	Mexican. Short knife.
WENDELL	Mexican short knife?

(FELIX nods)

WENDELL	Where the fuck you get that?

(FELIX shows WENDELL the bag containing the dead bird, which has been practically torn open)

WENDELL	What the fuck is that?
FELIX	Your. Dead rooster?
WENDELL	*(Knowing it is)* Christ.
FELIX	It was here. When I woke. Up.
WENDELL	Your son must really hate you.
FELIX	Connecticut. Cockfighting. Cops. Bad.
WENDELL	Guess that's what you get for putting him in an orphanage.
FELIX	I have half. A body working. I cannot. Speak right. I am wearing. A Mexican short knife. At a dog track. I am paying. For mistakes.

(Pause)

WENDELL	She doesn't want to have my baby, Felix.
FELIX	Well. At least. You still. Have Michael.
WENDELL	You gotta stop it with that. I'm just trying to live my life.
FELIX	He's. Good. Michael.
WENDELL	Can't believe he visited you. By himself.
FELIX	Michael knows. He knows, I don't care. About gayness.
WENDELL	Write down the recipe. Don't fuck with me. Like you did Floyd.
FELIX	He-hit-me.

WENDELL	He saved me many times. Because he hit people. Somehow, if you look at it a certain way, you deserved this shit. Just write it down. I'm gonna sit here and not give you any food till you do. I got a burger in my pocket.
FELIX	He hit me. Hard.
WENDELL	*(Handing **FELIX** a paper and pen)* Just write it down.

*(**FELIX** begins to write)*

WENDELL	This better be a good fucking recipe.
FELIX	It. Is great.
WENDELL	You want to come to the cockfight with me?
FELIX	Where is it?
WENDELL	Washington Heights.
FELIX	No. Floyd hates me. He-will. Hit-me-again. Take me home.
WENDELL	Felix?
FELIX	Yeah.
WENDELL	When we take you home, you're gonna give me your second set of bird knives, okay? You're gonna do that for me.
FELIX	Ok.

*(**WENDELL** takes the recipe from **FELIX**)*

WENDELL	*(Reading)* This is the recipe?

FELIX	Yes.
WENDELL	*(Reading)* Hartshorne?
FELIX	Get it. At the drug store. *(Handing **WENDELL** the short knife)* Here. Here is. Your short knife.
WENDELL	Thanks. *(Taking out the burger, biting into it, chewing)* If it's all right. I think I'm gonna cry now.

*(**WENDELL** does not cry)*

SCENE 8

Setting: That morning. The apartment.

*At rise, **GERONIMO** preparing for today's match, going through various things, his old knives, solvents, perhaps HE is even playing with the bird. **FLOYD**, who has obviously been up all night, is staring right at HIM. The couch still has unmade bed sheets on it.*

GERONIMO	Floyd.
FLOYD	What?
GERONIMO	Do not try and take my cash.
FLOYD	When?
GERONIMO	When we win. *(Holding out HIS hand)* Shake.
FLOYD	On what?
GERONIMO	On that you will not take my money.

(FLOYD shakes GERONIMO's hand)

FLOYD	I won't take your money. *(Beat)* It's a good thing you made me shake.
GERONIMO	Why?
FLOYD	'Cause I'm disgusting. 'Cause I can't control myself.
GERONIMO	*(Sniffing)* You smell funny.
FLOYD	Hey Geronimo.
GERONIMO	What?
FLOYD	Fuck you.

(WENDELL enters with a carton of eggs and a stick of butter. He crosses to the stove to make eggs)

FLOYD	We got a shitload to do, Wendell.
WENDELL	Well good, then you can feed them Felix's proper recipe finally.
FLOYD	You got it?
WENDELL	Yeah, I got it. And I got the fuckin' knives. I got the knives and the recipe. You ready for this? It's fucking instant coffee, ground up Corn Flakes, and diced orange peels. How can you NOT remember this? It's made from basic household products. Like your childhood breakfast cereal. It's so easy to make it makes me want to punch you and Felix in the face.
FLOYD	Corn Flakes sounds familiar.
WENDELL	Of course it does.

FLOYD *(Remembering)* Corn Flakes?

WENDELL Right, the oranges give the birds sugar, the coffee gives them caffeine, the combo makes them go bezerk.

FLOYD Totally forgot about the cornflakes.

WENDELL I guess that's why they put a rooster on the box. *(Beat)* What you probably wouldn't have remembered. Was the Hartshorne.

FLOYD Hartshorne.

GERONIMO *(Remembering)* Hartshorne. He. That is right.

WENDELL *(Sarcastic)* What would we do without you, Nimo. *(To **FLOYD**)* It's like a medieval yeast. Or it's ground from deer antlers. I don't fuckin' know. Can't believe you can buy it in a drugstore. *(Beat)* I'm so tired. Let's fucking make this thing.

FLOYD Wendell. I gotta tell you something. 'Cause you're my good good friend. You always took care a me.

WENDELL It's fine, man. It's what I do.

FLOYD I fucked your wife.

*(**FLOYD** stands and crosses to the kitchenette)*

FLOYD Sit down. I'll make these eggs for you.

*(**WENDELL** sits down. **FLOYD** lights the stove)*

GERONIMO   What?
FLOYD   Geronimo, shut up.

(FLOYD sprays Pam into a pan, then breaks three eggs into the skillet and lets' them cook for a very short period of time, barely to a point in which they are solid)

GERONIMO   Floyd.
FLOYD   Geronimo.

(FLOYD takes the barely cooked eggs, places them on a plate, sprinkles some salt and pepper on them, and places them in front of WENDELL)

FLOYD   I'm sorry. Here. I've made you some eggs.
WENDELL   Uh.
FLOYD   What.
WENDELL   Um.
FLOYD   What's the problem?
WENDELL   *(Referring to the eggs)* They're really runny.
FLOYD   They cook while they sit there.
WENDELL   You have to put them back in the pan. 'Cause they're not cooked enough to even try to cook while they sit here.
FLOYD   They'll become eggs like you know them in a minute. Let them cook on your plate.
WENDELL   If you put them back in the pan I think they'll cook better.
FLOYD   Pops used to do it like this.

WENDELL   *(Beat, to **FLOYD**)* Why'd you sleep with my wife?

FLOYD   She's pregnant already. It can't happen twice. I think she's been with a lot of men, lately, Wendell. I could smell it on her. I didn't think it was fair, the way she was treating you. She's sleeping in the other room. Go talk to her.

WENDELL   She was treating me fine. *(Beat)* These eggs are not cookin' while they sit here.

FLOYD   They will. Just hold out.

GERONIMO   I should leave.

*(**WENDELL** stands and crosses to the stove)*

FLOYD   Rosalind's just a waste of your time, Wendell. She's just a waste of your time.

*(With a growing rage, **WENDELL** picks up the pan)*

FLOYD   *(continued)* And you know what? No wonder Michael's gotten so chubby since puberty.

WENDELL   It's not my kid.

*(Perhaps in conjunction with the previous line, **WENDELL** smashes the pan on **FLOYD**'s skull. **FLOYD** falls down hard)*

WENDELL   *(continued) (To **FLOYD**)* Why can't a man just have a goddamn family for once? Why can't a man have a goddamn family?

SCENE 8 a (Optional)

Setting: That afternoon. The cockfight.

*At rise, spotlight up on **GERONIMO** and **WENDELL** with the ROOSTER, presumably in the cockfighting ring. **WENDELL** stands there reluctantly holding the cage as **GERONIMO** removes the ROOSTER from its pen, flaunts IT about, blows in IT's beak, and gets IT revved up for the fight. In disbelief, **WENDELL** slowly pulls the cage from the ring in disbelief as **GERONIMO** prepares to let the bird lose on IT's opponent.*

SCENE 8 b (Optional)

Setting: Early that evening. The apartment.

*At rise, **ROSALIND** enters and looks about at the tattered surroundings. SHE begins cleaning. By the time SHE is done, the apartment looks significantly more tidied than it did when SHE arrived.*

SCENE 9

Setting: Later that evening. The apartment.

At rise, money stacked very high in several piles on the kitchen table, even more on the coffee tables and couch. WENDELL is sitting at the table chewing on Wendy's chicken nuggets; an empty bag sits next to the meal. GERONIMO stands in the bathroom, starring at the ROOSTER, which is lying severely injured in the bathtub, out of view from the audience. IT is barely breathing.

WENDELL	Jesus Christ.
GERONIMO	He is barely alive, but he is alive.
WENDELL	That's Calagay?
GERONIMO	Yes. That is him.
WENDELL	Oh man.
GERONIMO	We should keep him in the bath. He is still bleeding.
WENDELL	Sure. *(Noticing the gash on the ROOSTER's face)* Did he lose an eye?
GERONIMO	Yeah. He did. The short knife has a very serious blade.
WENDELL	Nimo.
GERONIMO	What?
WENDELL	Should we just . . . he's dying.
GERONIMO	No. If we can keep him alive we can breed him.
WENDELL	But. He's dying.
GERONIMO	But what if he does not.

WENDELL	This is one hell of a way to pay your bills.
GERONIMO	Where is my money?
WENDELL	*(Referring to the money)* You're portion is over by the stove.

(GERONIMO stops and stares at his portion)

GERONIMO	That is a lot of fucking money. Per volume.
WENDELL	It's organized in easy-to-deposit piles.
GERONIMO	I do not think it would be so . . . so much.
WENDELL	Did you think it'd fit in your wallet?
GERONIMO	Ay nako. So much. *(Looking around the apartment, noticing it is cleaner)* Who cleaned?
WENDELL	Rosalind came over. I think.
GERONIMO	Oh.
WENDELL	While we were at the fight. Lina's over there. Love to hear that conversation.
GERONIMO	I never handled birds before, in a ring like that. I didn't think I'd be . . . good. When we lost the first fight. But man, after that. Three in a row. But when Calagay went down, I didn't get nervous, I stayed calm, just blew in his face, rubbed his beak. Then he destroyed that brown bird. *(Noticing the food-of-choice)* Are you eating chicken?
WENDELL	Yes.

GERONIMO Didn't you see the big bucket that said "Dead Roosters" pointing down?

WENDELL That was gross. *(Beat)* We won. *(Disbelief)* Calagay made that brown chicken spit up blood.

GERONIMO But he take it to the brain. Twice. He'll be okay.

WENDELL That chicken. It winning? Was supposed to put my life back together, Nimo. Isn't that funny?

GERONIMO In a short time, Floyd did a really good job conditioning these birds. What a talent. *(Beat)* What are you going to do with Floyd's money?

WENDELL Give it to him? That's what this whole thing was for, right? To get Floyd outta the house.

GERONIMO *(Beat, then as delicately as possible)* All of it? Wendell, he only had a hand in these birds for a little while.

WENDELL *(Beat)* What's that supposed to mean?

GERONIMO I don't know.

WENDELL I'd appreciate it if you wouldn't talk like that right now.

GERONIMO Wendell.

WENDELL What?

GERONIMO He wasn't even at the fight.

WENDELL So.

GERONIMO We're the ones who won.

WENDELL And he helped us train them.

GERONIMO   Yeah. And then he fucked your wife—
WENDELL   Hey—
GERONIMO   Yeah, what the fuck, give him his money—
WENDELL   Woah—
GERONIMO   Motherfucker fuck my wife I take a short knife to his throat.
WENDELLL   Watch your fuckin' mouth Nimo—
GERONIMO   While you're at it why don't you take Lina back too, let everybody continue to eat the shit you made—
WENDELL   You better shut the fuck up.
GERONIMO   It's a lot of money Wendell—
WENDELL   It belongs to people.
GERONIMO   Who? Floyd? Rosalind? Lina? You behave like these people care for you.
WENDELL   You got no idea what you're talkin' about your wife's been dead so long. *(Pause)* I'm sorry.
GERONIMO   *(Quietly, angrily, definitively)* Do NOT underestimate grief.
WENDELL   I don't wanna go to a cockfight again.
GERONIMO   The way you behaved there, that makes sense.
WENDELL   I'm a fucking good man, Nimo. I'm a good person.
GERONIMO   Yeah, Wendell. That got you real far. *(Crossing back to the bathtub, then trying to will the ROOSTER back to consciousness,*

lovingly, yet with a sense of directive) You're gonna make it bird.

SCENE 10

Setting: The apartment. About two weeks later.

At rise, the place looks very different. Many of the piles have been either removed or placed against the wall. **LINA**, *perhaps shaking a bit, looking very weak, is rocking the baby.* **THE CHILD** *is swaddled in pink.* **WENDELL** *is unpacking groceries near the refrigerator.*

LINA	*(To the CHILD)* Just sleep, honey. Just sleep.
WENDELL	She will.
LINA	Shh. She's getting there.
WENDELL	*(Beat)* How are you feeling?
LINA	You need to stop asking me that.
WENDELL	I'll stop. Asking. *(Referring to the CHILD)* How's she doing?
LINA	She's very small.
WENDELL	*(Referring to the groceries)* I got what you asked for.
LINA	Thanks.
WENDELL	You don't have to breast feed.
LINA	I'm breast feeding. I'm her mother.
WENDELL	You're low on energy.
LINA	I'm breast feeding.

WENDELL	*(Beat)* Okay.
LINA	Yeah.
WENDELL	Good. *(Beat)* There's formula. It's powdered. It's in the cabinet. If you need it—
LINA	Pour it down the toilet.
WENDELL	It'll be in the cabinet.

*(**WENDELL** places the bag in the cabinet. **LINA** is oblivious to this)*

WENDELL	You want something to drink or something? Like a cola?
LINA	No.
WENDELL	I'm tired.
LINA	*(Looking about the place)* Thanks for cleaning up. This place looks good.

*(**WENDELL** opens the refrigerator again. The entire unit is now filled with soft drinks. No alcohol is in sight. **WENDELL** takes out a cola, opens it, takes a sip, then takes a cold burger from the refrigerator and takes a bite)*

WENDELL	You guys look pretty calm. Sittin' there.
LINA	I don't feel that calm.
WENDELL	Well it's pretty calming. To look at the two of you.
LINA	At least somebody's calm.
WENDELL	You're like. We're like a big weird family.

(LINA admires the CHILD, then looks at WENDELL. After a moment, SHE actually smiles)

LINA	Do you think?
WENDELL	What?
LINA	We're like a big weird family?
WENDELL	Totally.
LINA	That's hilarious.
WENDELL	Why?
LINA	'Cause this is one fucked up family.
WENDELL	It is, isn't it?
LINA	Totally. *(Referring to the baby)* I just can't believe she is actually a real live baby.

(WENDELL shoves the rest of the burger in his mouth and chews until he can speak)

WENDELL	Wish that shit was good for you. That tasted awesome.
LINA	*(Ruminating)* A big weird family.
WENDELL	Totally.

(WENDELL, smiling, takes a big sip from his cola, finishes the can, then throws it out)

WENDELL   Lina. Did you never really love me?

(Long pause)

LINA   *(Meaning it)* I love you.

*(Beat. **WENDELL** smiles. **LINA** smiles, then turns back around to admire the CHILD. Then, without warning, HE falls over on the floor. Somehow, at first, **LINA** doesn't notice this, as if his fall was cushioned by a pillow)*

LINA *(Beat)* Wendell?

SCENE 11

Setting: Two weeks later. Stadium-style seats at the greyhound track in Bridgeport, CT.

*At rise, **FLOYD** holding a dog racing ticket in his hand. **LINA** sits with him, holding the CHILD.*

FLOYD	We should stop by and give my dad some money, since we're here.
LINA	That. That is your call. *(Beat)* I like your uniform.
FLOYD	Thanks. Nimo got new ones.
LINA	You look pretty handsome.
FLOYD	You know, everybody notices these things. It's weird. *(Beat)* He just fell over?
LINA	Uh-huh. I barely heard him fall.
FLOYD	He's a big guy.
LINA	I've been through a lot, Floyd.
FLOYD	He wasn't exactly the type of guy who was gonna die of old age.
LINA	Floyd—

FLOYD	Massive heart attack was practically written on his birth certificate.
LINA	Please. Floyd. Not today.
FLOYD	*(Actually apologising)* Ok. Sorry. Sometimes I can't stop myself.
LINA	I know. *(Beat)* Thanks for taking me out of the house.
FLOYD	No problem.
LINA	This, this isn't exactly what I had in mind, the dog track, but thank you.
FLOYD	It's the only place I know. That I feel calm.
LINA	Well I'd say that's a pretty weird phenomenon.

(The starting bell is heard)

FLOYD	*(Looking)* They come around the track fast.
LINA	*(Looking)* They're so skinny.
FLOYD	*(Flashing his ticket in the air)* C'mon FIVE, you motherfucker.
LINA	It's bad enough we're sitting with her at the dog track. Please don't curse.
FLOYD	*(Referring to the racing dogs again)* Five is totally gonna shit the bed.
LINA	Floyd.
FLOYD	Ok. Last curse. Swear.
LINA	*(Noticing his dog is losing)* You're a bad gambler.

FLOYD I just guessed wrong.

LINA You can raise a rooster, but you're a bad gambler.

FLOYD Well I'll try to do better with our champion rooster babies. I won everybody a lot of money, Lina.

LINA I know.

FLOYD I'd appreciate a thank you once in a while.

LINA Thank you.

FLOYD *(Beat)* Just wait till these birds hit again.

LINA Floyd. If it's okay. No more birds. For me.

FLOYD *(Hurt?)* Ok. *(Beat)* What if. The kid needs help?

LINA Floyd. She's not your kid.

FLOYD *(Beat)* If you try and be nice then I'll continue to try and be nice too.

LINA Ok. *(Beat)* If you want to focus on a kid, focus on Theo. He's a nice kid.

FLOYD *(Beat)* You think so?

LINA And Michael. For what its worth. He's... upstanding. You should be proud.

FLOYD I am. Of both of them.

LINA *(Beat)* Best if you not tell Rosalind about the money.

FLOYD I think she'd understand, Rosalind, if I told her.

LINA I don't think so.

FLOYD *(Beat, the referring to **WENDELL**)* I'm going to really really miss him.

LINA Me too.

FLOYD *(Pause, referring to the CHILD)* It's kind of weird. That he's inside of that, huh?

(LINA cannot really contain her sadness at this idea. SHE turns away to not let FLOYD see HER upset)

FLOYD	Lina?
LINA	What?
FLOYD	When you gonna name the baby?
LINA	What?
FLOYD	She should have a name. It's been a long time.
LINA	I can't decide. With Wendell and everything.
FLOYD	I just call her baby. It's kind of demented. *(Beat)* You gotta name her.
LINA	What?
FLOYD	What?
LINA	What do I name her?
FLOYD	I don't know. You're the mom.
LINA	I don't know what to name her.
FLOYD	Name her after your mother, I don't know.
LINA	Are you kidding me?
FLOYD	This is sick, Lina. The child should have a name.
LINA	You name her.
FLOYD	It's not my baby.
LINA	You should help me name her something.
FLOYD	Oh no, don't do that to me.

LINA	Well then she won't have a name for a little longer. Watch your race.
FLOYD	It's over. I lost.
LINA	Then wait for the next one. *(Beat)* Pass me the bottle.
FLOYD	*(Doing so)* Thought you were breast feeding.
LINA	I am. It's in the bottle.
FLOYD	You can do that?
LINA	For several decades now we've been able to do this.
FLOYD	Oh.

(FLOYD watches LINA feed the CHILD. Beat)

FLOYD	How about Isabelle?
LINA	What?
FLOYD	Is Isabelle a nice name?
LINA	*(Considering)* Why Isabelle?
FLOYD	'Cause she is…
LINA	What?
FLOYD	'Cause she… is a bell.
LINA	*(Considering some more)* Isabelle.
FLOYD	Or something. I don't know. Name the fucking human being.
LINA	Isabelle.
FLOYD	That's the only girl name in my arsenal.
LINA	Isabelle.
FLOYD	Run it by the girls at Macy's girls. Take a vote.

LINA	Isabelle.
FLOYD	I don't want to be responsible for this. Decide for yourself. I'm simply an advisor. *(Looking at the CHILD)* She is pretty cute, though. If little.
LINA	She's like, a little unit of a human.
FLOYD	*(Tearing?)* Please stop. *(Beat)* If you ever need anything, Lina. Like to get out of the house, like we've done today. Just know you can come to me. Just know that. I'll try and keep this job for as long I can. Rosalind will just have to understand.
LINA	Thanks Floyd. But I'm fine. *(Then, regarding **WENDELL**? Regarding leaving the park?)* What are we gonna do?
FLOYD	I don't know. *(Beat)* I'd just like to sit for a second. Before we go.
LINA	We're going?
FLOYD	Yeah. I'd just like to sit for a second, though.
LINA	Ok.
FLOYD	In quiet. I'd just like to sit quiet for a second. In quiet.

(THEY sit in quiet for about ten seconds)

END OF PLAY